LANGUAGE ARTS EXPLORER JUNIOR

Verbs

run

grow

play

by Josh Gregory

D1418275

CHERRY LAKE PUBLISHING · ANN ARBOR, MICHIGAN

CHERRY LAKE

Publishing

A note on the text: Certain words are highlighted as examples of verbs.

Bold, colorful words are vocabulary words and can be found in the glossary.

Published in the United States of America by Cherry Lake Publishing
Ann Arbor, Michigan
www.cherrylakepublishing.com

Content Adviser: Lori Helman, PhD, Associate Professor, Department of Curriculum & Instruction, University of Minnesota, Minneapolis, Minnesota

Photo Credits: Page 4, ©Thai Soriano/Shutterstock, Inc.; page 6, ©Hannamariah/Shutterstock, Inc.; page 13, ©Kzenon/Shutterstock, Inc.; page 16, ©l i g h t p o e t/Shutterstock, Inc.; page 17, ©muzsy/Shutterstock, Inc.; page 20, ©Erik Lam/Shutterstock, Inc.

Library of Congress Cataloging-in-Publication Data
Gregory, Josh.
  Verbs / By Josh Gregory.
    pages cm. — (Language Arts Explorer Junior)
  Includes bibliographical references and index.
  ISBN 978-1-62431-179-6 (lib. bdg.) —
  ISBN 978-1-62431-245-8 (e-book) — ISBN 978-1-62431-311-0 (pbk.)
  1. English language—Verb—Juvenile literature. 2. English language—Parts of speech—Juvenile literature. 3. English language—Grammar—Juvenile literature. I. Title.
  PE1271.G74 2013
  428.2—dc23   2013007653

Cherry Lake Publishing would like to acknowledge the work of The Partnership for 21st Century Skills. Please visit www.p21.org for more information.

Printed in the United States of America
Corporate Graphics Inc.
July 2013
CLFA13

Table of Contents

CHAPTER ONE

A New Best Friend

Alex could not wait to see his dad's surprise.

Alex's dad cracked the front door open and peeked his head inside. "I've got a surprise for you," he said.

"What is it?" Alex asked with excitement. He set down the book he was reading and rushed toward the door.

"See for yourself," Alex's dad replied. He opened the door the rest of the way. Suddenly, a furry, brown blur burst into the house.

"It's a puppy!" Alex shouted. "I can't believe it!"

"I know you've been wanting one," Alex's dad replied. "You will have to work hard to take care of him."

"No problem," said Alex. "I will feed him, walk him, and everything else!"

Alex and his dad used many verbs when discussing the new puppy. Verbs are words that describe what people or things do, such as "he works," "she jumps," or "it falls." These are action verbs. Verbs also describe how something is, such as "the flower is red." Verbs are one of the most important parts of speech. There is at least one verb in every complete sentence.

The puppy jumped into Alex's lap and began to lick Alex's face. "His fur feels so soft," Alex said as he petted the dog.

"What will his name be?" Alex's dad asked.

Alex scrunched up his face as he thought about it. "Well," he said, "the puppy is brown. I guess I will call him Brownie."

"Brownie seems like a good name to me," Alex's dad replied.

There are many fun things to do with a new puppy.

Extra Examples

You cannot simply memorize which verbs are linking verbs and which are action verbs. Many verbs can be used both ways! Here are some examples:

Verb	Action	Linking
Smelled	She smelled the flower.	The flower smelled good.
Grew	He grew potatoes.	The potatoes grew big.
Looked	He looked out the window.	The window looked dirty.
Tasted	She tasted the soup.	The soup tasted good.

Most verbs are action verbs. But sometimes verbs connect the **subject** of a sentence to that subject's description. These verbs are called linking verbs.

"We should talk about what you need to do to take care of Brownie," Alex's dad said. "You must remember to feed him every day. You should feed him once in the morning and once at night."

"Got it!" Alex replied.

"You need to walk him at least once every day," Alex's dad continued. "You can walk him more than that, if you want to."

Some verbs are joined with other verbs to give them a certain meaning. These verbs are known as helping verbs. They don't mean much by themselves. However, they can greatly change the meaning of a sentence. For example, "I must eat" means something different than "I should eat."

To get a copy of this activity, visit www.cherrylakepublishing.com/activities.

ACTIVITY

Locate and List

List all the helping verbs you can find in the following sentences:

"You will also clean up after Brownie when he goes to the bathroom," Alex's dad told him. "I do not want to find any messes in the yard."

"I will try to clean up after him," Alex replied, "but I might forget sometimes."

"I hope you are kidding," Alex's dad said, "because I do not think that is funny!"

Answers:

"You **will** also clean up after Brownie when he goes to the bathroom," Alex's dad told him. "I **do** not want to find any messes in the yard."

"I **will** try to clean up after him," Alex replied, "but I **might** forget sometimes."

"I hope you **are** kidding," Alex's dad said, "because I **do** not think that is funny!"

CHAPTER TWO

Today, Tomorrow, Yesterday

Brownie hopped out of Alex's lap. The tiny dog began zipping around the room.

"He runs fast!" Alex shouted as he chased Brownie. "I can't catch him!"

"He is definitely quick," Alex's dad agreed. "You are no match for him."

Verbs can explain things that are a certain way right now. This is called the present **tense**.

"He is moving as fast as lightning," Alex said. "Look how he is dodging around me when I try to grab him!"

Sometimes an action is **ongoing**, or keeps going. Verbs look a little different when they describe these actions. They end in *-ing*.

They are also connected to helping verbs. For example, a person might say, "Brownie runs." To make the sentence describe ongoing action, a person might say, "Browning is running." The verb *run* becomes *running*, with the helping verb *is* added before it.

ACTIVITY

Read and Rethink

Rewrite the following sentences. Change the present tense action verbs in red to their ongoing form.

Suddenly, Brownie stopped running. "Look," said Alex. "He wags his tail!"

"Watch out," Alex's dad answered. "He gets ready to run again!"

Answers:
Suddenly, Brownie stopped running. "Look," said Alex.
"He is wagging his tail!"
"Watch out," Alex's dad answered. "He is getting ready to run again!"

To get a copy of this activity, visit www.cherrylakepublishing.com/activities.

"It's time for you and Brownie to go to bed," Alex's dad said. "Tomorrow will be a busy day. You will need plenty of rest."

"I will miss Brownie when I'm at school tomorrow," Alex said.

"Brownie will wait for you here at home," his dad answered.

Verbs can also describe things that will happen later. This is called the future tense. Future tense verbs can be made by adding *will* in front of them.

"He is going to be so happy when I get home," said Alex.

"Yes he will," Alex's dad replied. "Now go to bed."

To talk about what you will do in the future, such as going to school the next day, you need the future tense.

"OK," said Alex. "Brownie and I are going to sleep now."

You can also form the future tense by a helping verb and the words *going to*.

"Goodnight, Brownie," Alex said as he went up to his bedroom. "I will be thinking about you all day tomorrow!"

Future tense verbs can also be ongoing. Like ongoing present tense verbs, they end in *-ing*. The words *will be* are placed before an ongoing future tense verb.

The next day at school, Alex told his friend Luke about Brownie. "I named the puppy Brownie because I noticed his brown fur," Alex said.

Verbs can describe things that happened in the past. Usually, *-ed* is added to the end of the present tense verb to make it past tense. For example, *name* changes to *named*, and *notice* becomes *noticed*.

"Does Brownie know any tricks?" Luke asked.

"Not yet," Alex answered. "Last night he just ran around after my dad brought him home." Not all past tense verbs are formed by adding -ed. Some are **irregular**. For example, the present tense verb *run* becomes *ran. Bring* is changed to *brought*.

"Brownie and I were playing for a long time," said Alex. "I was petting him. Then he jumped on the floor."

Ongoing past tense verbs, just like ongoing

present tense verbs, need a helping verb. Ongoing past tense verbs have *were* or *was* in front of them.

ACTIVITY

Locate and List

Read the following sentences. Then list all of the action verbs you notice. Sort them into past, present, and future tense groups.

After school, Alex jogged home as fast as he could. He pushed the front door open. Brownie launched toward him as he walked inside. "Dad, I am going outside with Brownie!" he yelled.

   "Don't forget to put on his leash first," his dad called back.

   "I am clipping it onto his collar right now," Alex replied. "We will be back in a little while!"

Answers:
past: jogged, pushed, launched, walked, said, yelled, called, replied
present: forget, put, am clipping
future: am going, will be

To get a copy of this activity, visit www.cherrylakepublishing.com/activities.

CHAPTER THREE

Other Verbs

People use many different verbs when training dogs.

"Follow me," Alex said. He gently tugged on Brownie's leash. The dog wagged his tail and trotted along at Alex's side. "It's time for you to start learning some tricks," said Alex. He stopped walking and patted Brownie on the backside. "Sit," he commanded. Brownie looked up at him. He moved his head to the side. Alex pushed again on Brownie's backside. The dog suddenly understood what Alex wanted. He sat down. "Good boy!" Alex said with a smile. "Now roll over." Brownie began scratching himself. "Hmm," said Alex. "I guess we need to work on that one a little."

Verbs can be used to give instructions or commands. These verbs are usually the first word in a sentence. The subject of a command verb is always "you." However, it might not always be written or said aloud. For example, when Alex says "Sit" to Brownie, he means, "You sit."

Coaches, teachers, and your parents may often use command verbs.

"Let's go inside now," Alex said to Brownie. "I'm getting hungry. Aren't you?" Brownie barked in reply and followed Alex into the house.

"It's a good thing you came back in now," Alex's dad said. "Dinner is just about ready."

"What're we having?" Alex asked.

"You'll see soon enough," his dad replied. "Don't forget to feed Brownie and give him clean water."

Verbs can be combined with other words to form contractions. In a contraction, a verb is placed next to another word. Some of the letters are replaced with an **apostrophe**. For example, *don't* is formed from the words *do not*. *Let's* is formed by the words *let us*.

To get a copy of this activity, visit www.cherrylakepublishing.com/activities.

ACTIVITY

Read and Rethink

Read the following sentences. Then rewrite them, changing the verbs in red into contractions.

1. "You are doing a great job taking care of Brownie," Alex's dad said as they sat down at the dinner table.
2. "He is a great dog," Alex replied. "I am so happy you got him for me."
3. "You should have seen the look on your face when I opened the door last night," said Alex's dad.
4. "I did not expect a dog to run into the house!" Alex responded.

Answers:
1. You're
2. He's, I'm
3. should've
4. didn't

Dogs love to chew on toys.

After dinner, Alex and his dad went into the living room. Brownie followed behind them.

"Here," said Alex's dad. "I picked up a toy for Brownie today." He held up a short rope with handles on each end.

"Thanks!" Alex exclaimed. "Here, boy!" he called to Brownie. The dog scampered over. "Let's play tug-of-war," said Alex. He showed the toy to Brownie. Brownie immediately snatched one end of the rope in his teeth. He began yanking on it. Alex laughed as he struggled to win the game.

"I wonder who will win," his dad said as he watched them play.

ACTIVITY

Read and Rethink!

Read the following sentences, and then rewrite them, filling in the missing verbs. Be creative and keep tense in mind.

Finally, Brownie _____ the toy out of Alex's hands. "You _____," Alex said as he _____ backward. "But we _____ again tomorrow!" Brownie _____ his tail.

"Why don't you _____ him a treat?" _____ Alex's dad. Alex _____ over to the kitchen. He _____ the box of treats.

"_____," Alex commanded. To his surprise, the dog _____ right away. "Wow!" _____ Alex. "You _____ a fast learner!"

To get a copy of this activity, visit www.cherrylakepublishing.com/activities.

Glossary

apostrophe (uh-PAHS-truh-fee) the punctuation mark used to show letters that have been left out

irregular (ir-REG-yuh-lur) not following the normal rules or pattern

ongoing (AWN-goh-ing) still happening or developing

subject (SUHB-jikt) a word or group of words in a sentence that tells who or what is doing the action expressed by the verb

tense (TENS) a form of a verb that shows whether an action happened in the past, is happening in the present, or will happen in the future

For More Information

BOOKS

Cleary, Brian P. *Slide and Slurp, Scratch and Burp: More About Verbs.* Minneapolis: Millbrook Press, 2007.

Cook, Julia. *It's Hard to Be a Verb!* Chattanooga, TN: National Center for Youth Issues, 2008.

WEB SITES

Between the Lions—Word Play
http://pbskids.org/lions/games/wordplay.html
Learn some new verbs with this fun interactive Web site.

HMH School Publishers—Verb Power
www.harcourtschool.com/activity/verb_power/index_pre.html
Play this game to learn more about main verbs, helping verbs, and contractions.

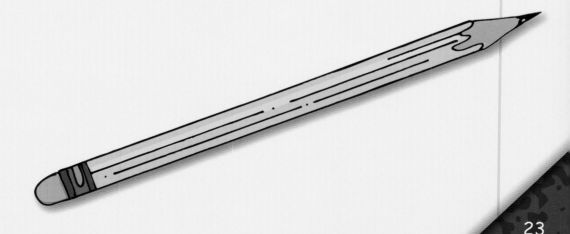

Index

About the Author

Josh Gregory writes and edits books for kids. He lives in Chicago, Illinois.

DEC 2013

LANGUAGE ARTS
EXPLORER JUNIOR

The ability to recognize and correctly use the different parts of speech is key to developing strong writing skills. In this series, readers will follow exciting storylines to learn about the roles different types of words play in sentences. Activity sidebars help teach concepts such as tense and correct punctuation.

Read all the books in this series:
Adjectives
Adverbs
Conjunctions
Interjections
Nouns
Prepositions
Pronouns
Verbs

CHERRY LAKE Publishing

GR: M

ISBN-13: 978-1624313110

9 781624 313110

T2-DBW-739

Harlequin ducks swim in rivers with fast **currents**. They dive to the bottom to catch **insects**. Sometimes, they use their strong **bills** to eat snails, crabs, and mussels.

 # Living Over the Water

Willow flycatchers build their nests in tall bushes and short trees. Sometimes, they live on islands in rivers. They eat a lot of **insects** while flying.

Ospreys often build their nests in tall trees near rivers or on islands in wide rivers. Some ospreys nest on large rocks in the middle of rivers!

 # Finding Food in a River

Paddlefishes live on the muddy bottoms of rivers with slow **currents.** They eat very tiny plants and animals that live in the river.

Mergansers are ducks that swim under the water to catch fishes. The sides of a merganser's **bill** look like a saw. This helps them hold on to the fish.

 # River Predators

Some river animals are **predators.** They hunt other animals for food. The alligator gar is a fish. Its strong mouth can crush other fishes and small **mammals.**

Alaskan brown bears come to rivers to catch salmon. They swim in the water and fish. Then, they quickly eat the salmon.

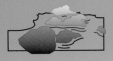 # Hiding in a River

Water dogs are salamanders that live
on river bottoms. They usually have spots
that help them blend in with the rocks.
They like to hide under rocks and logs.

Harter's water snakes live in deep rivers with fast **currents.** They come onto the **river bank** to lie in the sun and hide under rocks.

 River Babies

Mother salmon come to rivers to lay eggs. She lays eggs in a hole in the river bottom. After the eggs **hatch,** the young fishes look for **insects** and plants to eat.

Caddisfly **larvae** often live underwater or along the edge of a river. They make a net to catch small animals to eat from the moving water.

 # Protecting River Animals

Sometimes people put trash or **harmful chemicals** in rivers. Some companies put very hot water in rivers. Big boats that move fast make waves that crash into **river banks** and **erode** them.

These things harm river plants and animals.
Let's keep our rivers clean and protect
river animals from danger. When you visit
a river, put your trash in a garbage can.

# **Glossary**

bill mouth of a bird

burrow to dig

current movement of water in one direction down a river

erode to wear dirt away

glacier big piece of ice that slowly moves down a mountain or across land

habitat place where an animal lives

harmful chemical thing that can kill plants and animals

hatch to come out of an egg

insect small animal with six legs

larva (more than one are called larvae) very young insect

lodge beaver home

mammal animal, like humans, that has a backbone and hair or fur

predator animal that hunts and eats other animals

river bank land beside a river

surface top of a river or other body of water

web sheet of skin that fills the space between toes

More Books to Read

Ashwell, Miranda and Andy Owen. *Rivers.* Chicago: Heinemann Library, 1998.

Giesecke, Ernestine. *River Plants.* Chicago: Heinemann Library, 1999.

Robinson, Claire. *Bears.* Chicago: Heinemann Library, 1998.

# Index